DIGITAL AND INFORMATION LITERACY ™

BLOGS

FINDING YOUR VOICE, FINDING YOUR AUDIENCE

ARIE KAPLAN

rosen publishing's
rosen
central

New York

Published in 2012 by The Rosen Publishing Group, Inc.
29 East 21st Street, New York, NY 10010

Library of Congress Cataloging-in-Publication Data

Kaplan, Arie.
Blogs: finding your voice, finding your audience/Arie Kaplan.—1st ed.
    p. cm.—(Digital information and literacy)
Includes bibliographical references and index.
ISBN 978-1-4488-5556-8 (library binding)—
ISBN 978-1-4488-5618-3 (pbk.)—
ISBN 978-1-4488-5619-0 (6-pack)
1. Blogs—Juvenile literature. I. Title.
TK5105.8884.K37 2012
006.7'52—dc23

                                                            2011025288

Manufactured in the United States of America

CPSIA Compliance Information: Batch #W12YA: For further information, contact Rosen Publishing, New York, New York, at 1-800-237-9932.

CONTENTS

INTRODUCTION

A blog is a venue for self-expression that can be filled with different kinds of content. It can include collections of links to Web sites or other blogs that you like, funny stories about one's family, commentary on the news of the day, fashion tips, or even silly jokes and videos. It can be a personal space in which people make their voices heard.

These people aren't all teens, but teens naturally gravitate toward the blogosphere. In fact, chances are that if you don't have a blog of your own, someone else you know does. Ever wonder why that is? For one thing, a blog is easy to create. Furthermore, it doesn't cost anything to establish or maintain a blog. You are the performer, the writer, the director, and the crew. The audience is all of your readers (or followers) in cyberspace.

Since the late 1990s, blogging has changed the way we communicate. As a medium of personal expression, it has altered the way we share our innermost thoughts, experiences, and reactions. Blogs are forums for our most impassioned opinions and ideas. They are to the twenty-first century what diaries and journals were to previous eras. For this reason, blogging is most definitely a positive phenomenon, one that can enrich your life and make you feel more in tune with yourself and the world around you.

If you write with a sense of caution and responsibility—not to mention creativity and passion—blogging can be a highly rewarding activity.

But that doesn't mean that there aren't some dangers inherent in blogging. For example, there is the risk of oversharing, of accidentally providing personal information to those who would use it to hurt you, and of exposing yourself to flaming/bullying. Think before you blog. Remember, anything you post remains accessible in cyberspace indefinitely. What you dash off in a moment of haste, anger, or passion you may come to reget quickly— and forever. The permanence of your posts can make blogging seem like a daunting task. However, if you take care and write not only with spirit and creativity but also with a sense of caution and personal responsibility, blogging can be an exhilarating and highly rewarding activity.

Chapter 1

Why Blog?

Blogging is quick, easy, fun, and economical. So is there any question why teens flock to the blogosphere? There they can write creatively; document their daily lives; weigh in on the latest books, movies, or music; or express their most personal thoughts, hopes, fears, and dreams. There are even success stories of teens who have used blogging to become famous.

Teen Blogging Sensations

Tavi Gevinson, a teen blogger based in Chicago, Illinois, became a well-known style maven and a high-profile fixture at fashion shows due to her *Style Rookie* blog. Shortly after starting *Style Rookie* in 2008, when she was only eleven years old, Gevinson was featured in the *New York Times*. She was quickly placed in the coveted front row at New York Fashion Week shows.

Like any good blogger, Gevinson has a witty writing style, and she really understands and cares deeply about her subject. Most important, she has something to say, with a strong viewpoint and distinctive voice, and she isn't afraid to be brutally honest. Her fearlessly opinionated blog posts have won her a place of honor at fashion's runways. Gevinson's blog is

Chicago-based teen blogger Tavi Gevinson has become a high-profile fixture at fashion shows due to her popular, intelligent, and insightful *Style Rookie* blog.

so influential that, though she is still a high school student, fashion fans and industry insiders alike listen to and value her opinions. This is all a blogger of any age could hope for.

Nick Normile, from Philadelphia, Pennsylvania, started his blog, *Foodie at Fifteen*, when he was (you guessed it) fifteen. The blog chronicles his obsessions and musings about all things culinary. These include some of Normile's own quirky recipes, like "candy blondies." This is more or less a traditional blondie recipe, except that in this case, the blondies are bursting with chunks of Reese's peanut butter cups, Snickers, and candy corn.

File   Edit   View   Favorites   Tools   Help

BIRTH OF THE BLOG

Birth of the Blog

Do you know the origin of the word "blog"? Because the first real wave of bloggers started cropping up at roughly the same time, it's hard to say exactly who the first blogger was. But we do know this: Around 1997, there was a spurt of online activity, as various enterprising people fashioned what might be called the first real blogs. The thing that set these sites apart from others is that they all adhered to the same format, consisting of links with the blogger's running commentary. The most recent commentary—or "blog posts"—appeared first, with the older posts following downward in reverse chronological order.

Jorn Barger was the first person to coin the term "Weblog," which eventually was shortened to "blog."

Although these early commentary sites were blogs, the word "blog" wasn't coined until January 1999. This was when Cameron Barrett, who maintained the site *Camworld* (an early blog), wrote an essay titled "Anatomy of a Weblog," which described the type of site he maintained. Barrett didn't actually coin the term "Weblog," however. That was the work of Jorn Barger, who created the blog *Robot Wisdom*. All Barger did was combine two existing words, "Web" and "log," but it caught on. Soon, people all over the world were creating their own Weblogs, and the word "Weblog" was eventually shortened to "blog." By 2002, blogging became a bona fide phenomenon.

As a result of his work as a blogger, Normile was given five-star service at the New York restaurant Per Se. He has also received praise from *Philadelphia Magazine* and from noted food writer Michael Ruhlman. Like Gevinson, Normile creates posts that are not just about his chosen field (in his case, the culinary arts) but also about the larger world outside his immediate surroundings and interests and how it affects him.

Gevinson and Normile have several things in common. As teen bloggers, they have gained a surprising amount of attention, respect, and influence. They have made their highly distinctive and unique voices heard, while writing about their particular passions. They have also created worldwide connections with working professionals in the fields they write about, as well as with legions of fellow food and fashion devotees and loyal and appreciative blog followers.

Adults relate to these teen bloggers because they have something to say, something that's universal, and they say it with intelligence and courage. Teens relate to these bloggers because the writers have wants, needs, and opinions in common with them. The audience for Gevinson's and Normile's blogs—and those of other talented teen bloggers—isn't limited to one set demographic. These teen bloggers blog for everyone.

It's All About You (in a Good Way)

A blog is, first and foremost, a place for personal expression. You can post almost anything that you want on your blog (within the bounds of proper cyber-etiquette and good taste). Many people post journal-style entries, in which they explore whatever they happen to be feeling that very minute. This is exciting because both the blogger and those reading the blog are caught up in the immediacy and intensity of the moment. The blogger is making a sort of unspoken pact with his or her readership. The implied pact is that this blog will be a place of complete, direct, and unvarnished honesty.

Of course, some blogs don't take themselves quite that seriously, but for those that do, blogging functions as a forum for candor and openness. They also often alternate between diary-style posts (about what's going on in the

A blog can be a place to display your portfolio, whether you're a painter, a writer, a musician, a filmmaker, or a photographer.

blogger's personal life) and samples of short stories, art projects, sketches, photos, poetry, and music. Think of these more personal, confessional blogs as a sort of "museum of you," a living and ongoing self-portrait, or a virtual portfolio.

AOI Blogs

You shouldn't get the idea that people use blogging only as a way to vent about the minute details of their personal lives or share their latest creative writing. Sure, some blogs function in this capacity. However, many others do not. Many bloggers use their time in the blogosphere to share information about their niche interests or obsessions. Just for the sake of easy reference, let's call these types of blogs "areas of interest" blogs, or AOI blogs. The different types of AOI blogs are many and varied.

For example, a common type of AOI blog is one that focuses on reviews and articles about movies, TV shows, books, video games, theater, music, painting, and other forms of artistic expression. When you blog to express your opinion about a cultural or consumer product—whether it's a movie, a painting, a comic book, an album, or a new smartphone or app—your readers will rely on you to write in an entertaining, punchy style.

MYTH The quality of your blog posts doesn't matter because nobody's reading them anyway.

FACT While it might be true that you don't have very many readers, at least initially, it could also be true that your readers may eventually number in the thousands or even the millions. Therefore, the quality of your blog posts definitely matters. You should respect your audience, the craft of writing, and yourself as a writer enough to provide high-quality content, whether one person or one million people are reading.

MYTH Blogging is not "real writing."

FACT Blogging is most definitely real writing, and it's just as valid a form of writing as literary fiction and nonfiction, poetry, screenwriting, journalism, autobiography, or playwriting.

MYTH When I'm working on a blog, I should channel all of my time and energy into making it the greatest blog possible.

FACT While it's true that you should put a good deal of care into your blog, it's also true that you need balance in your life. You can't be completely focused on the blog 100 percent of the time. For one thing, if you never get outside and experience life, what will you have to blog about?

Chapter 2

How to Blog and Build an Audience

So far, we've discussed what sort of subject matter you should write about on your blog, but how do you actually go about setting up your blog in the first place? The task may seem daunting at first, but constructing your blog need not be an arduous task at all. It can even be fun!

Platform Diving

First, you must decide what blogging platform to choose. There are quite a few possibilities to consider. Two of the most popular blogging platforms are Blogger and WordPress. Blogger (aka Blogspot) is a free platform, and it's run by Google. It's great for beginning bloggers, and its set-up wizard is easy to use. In fact, using Blogger, you can create and activate your blog in just a few minutes. Blogger also gives you the option of owning your own domain name (in other words, your ".com" name). Also, its tabs and buttons are easy to navigate. And if you're proficient in CSS and HTML, you can customize your template to make it look flashier.

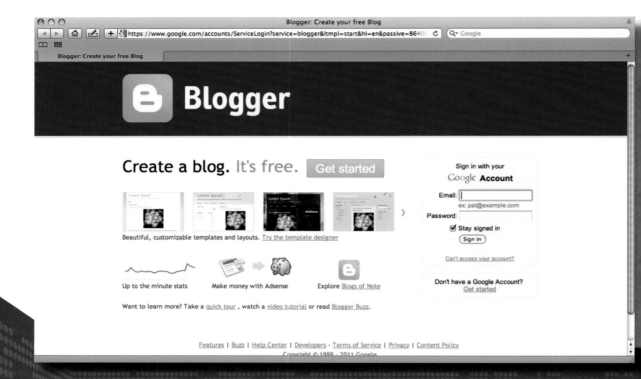

Blogger (aka Blogspot; http://www.blogger.com) is a free blogging platform, and it's great for beginning bloggers.

WordPress is one of the most well-known blogging software options out there. There are actually two types of WordPress software: WordPress.com, which is hosted, and WordPress.org, which is installable. When something is said to be "installable," that means that you place it on your own Web server.

What's in a Name?

Once you've decided what blogging platform you'll be using, you should probably decide what you'll call your blog. This might sound like a minor issue, but it really isn't. Names are important; they determine how we identify ourselves to others. Names have power and purpose. In the case of blogs, names can signal to readers your interests, tone, and style.

Naming your blog really comes down to a few basic considerations. For one, what will your blog be about? Will it be about pop culture (or any specific facet of pop culture, such as movies or music)? Will it be about cooking? Or fashion? Or sports? Or politics? Also, what is the target audience that you are trying to reach with your blog? Is your blog meant to appeal to indie rock fans, foodies, gamers, ballet enthusiasts, action figure collectors, or film buffs? What word—or combination of words—would best express what you're trying to say with your blog? Answering these questions will point you in the right direction and help you to come up with a blog title that feels true to you and your writing.

When you name your blog, try to pick a title that describes the blog in a really simple, direct, accurate, and maybe even amusing manner.

Templates: Designing the Look of Your Blog

After you've chosen a title for your blog, you need to select a template. A template is a framework designed to enhance the appearance of your site. It's like an all-in-one hair, makeup, and wardrobe department for your blog. A template is also used to enhance the usability of the site; it helps to make your blog look better, and it helps to make it easier to use.

There are many Web sites that offer users free blog templates that make designing and organizing a visually attractive blog quick and easy.

Many blog hosts offer generic templates for you to choose from when first starting your blog. Also, many Web designers create custom templates for blogs, and already designed (or "predesigned") templates are available on a variety of Web sites. However, that's not to say that you can't do a little tinkering with your blog template on your own. If you're familiar with HTML, you can change your link colors, banner, and other key visuals so that they better match the tone or subject matter of your site. For example, if your blog is about the Old West, your banner can show a public domain image of the iconic vistas of Monument Valley, where many famous Hollywood westerns were filmed.

The Sum of a Blog's Parts

You'll have to familiarize yourself with some basic blogging terminology and mechanics before you start blogging in earnest. What component parts does a blog consist of? These are the features that you'll find on pretty much any blog.

- **Posts (aka "entries"):** Each and every time you update your blog—whether you write the words "This is me blogging. Hi world!" or something lengthier and more in depth—you're creating a blog post, or entry, which you then add to the blog. Posts are the heart and soul of your blog.
- **Archives:** As a blogger, you'll usually sort your blog posts into an archive. The posts will be sorted by date, from most recent to oldest, to help readers (and you) find the newest posts or specific older posts more easily.
- **Comments:** Most likely, your blog will allow its readers to leave comments as a way to respond to your posts. What are comments? Essentially, they're short messages, and they're one of the features that differentiate a blog from other kinds of Web sites. They also encourage interactivity and an ongoing dialogue with your readers. The ability for a writer to connect directly with his or her readers—to receive feedback, share interests, and trade information—is one of the most exciting and innovative aspects of blogging.
- **Blogrolls:** If there's another blog that you find particularly interesting, chances are you'll include it on your blogroll, which is a list of

Writers can promote their blogs and create buzz by making use of social media tools like (from top to bottom) RSS feeds, Twitter, Facebook, and e-mail.

other noteworthy blogs. By including the blogs and Web sites that you like to read on your own blog, you can direct your readers to other interesting sites. Also, there's a chance that those other Web sites might return the favor, sending their readers to your site.

File   Edit   View   Favorites   Tools   Help

    BLOGS GO HOLLYWOOD

Blogs Go Hollywood

Today, Hollywood studios and book publishing companies sometimes troll through blogs to snatch up fresh, talented voices and find new ideas and material. This doesn't happen every day, but when it does happen, it definitely creates a media sensation.

For example, screenwriter Diablo Cody's career began after a movie producer contacted her and told her that he found her blogging style funny and clever. Shortly afterward, Cody wrote the screenplay for the movie *Juno*. Another example is provided by Robert Rummel-Hudson, who had written his blog, *Fighting Monsters with Rubber Swords*, since 1995. The blog deals almost exclusively with his daughter Schuyler, who suffers from polymicrogyria, a brain disorder that makes her unable to speak. The blog's tagline is "Schuyler is my weird and wonderful monster-slayer. Together we have many adventures." In 2008, Rummel-Hudson parlayed the popularity of his sensitive, insightful, and moving blog into a critically acclaimed book entitled *Schuyler's Monster*.

The synergy between mass media and blogging doesn't end there. Various TV shows have companion blogs, which are written in the voice of the show's characters. For example, if you like *The Office*, there's *Schrute Space*, written in the voice of the fictional paper salesman Dwight Schrute (played by Rainn Wilson). There, you can find blog posts in which Dwight tells you about his New Year's resolutions, his family recipes, and more. The ability to expand on a fictional universe—and to reward long-term fans of those universes—is just one of the many wonderful gifts that blogging offers readers and writers alike.

- **RSS feeds:** RSS stands for Really Simple Syndication. It's pretty much exactly what it sounds like. RSS is a simple way to syndicate, or distribute, your content (e.g., blog posts and podcasts) to your Web audience. RSS feeds help you to promote your blog, and they help potential readers gain access to it. With the help of RSS, code can be used to easily display your blog's feed on any number of other Web sites, including other blogs, search engines, and news aggregator sites. News aggregator sites use RSS to pull in and post topical stories from multiple Web sources. As a blogger, using RSS will boost traffic to your site and increase its exposure.

Generating Traffic and Finding Your Audience

OK, your blog is up and running, and you've taken your first tentative steps into the blogosphere. Now what? The next step is to find out who's reading your blog and how your readers found out about your blog in the first place. To do this, set up a stat counter on your blog. A stat counter is exactly what it sounds like: it counts statistics, in this case, how many visitors have checked out your blog. There are many free, user-friendly counters out there. They all come with easy-to-follow directions, showing you how to install them on your blog. Three of the most popular counters are Stat Counter, Google Analytics, and Site Meter.

Once your stat counter is set up, it's time to start generating traffic to your blog and give the stat counter something to count. Many blogs do this by establishing regular gimmicks or formulas (for example, a specialized weekly post that readers know to look for every Tuesday). This keeps visitors coming back for more, for the same reason TV viewers tune in on the same night every week to catch their favorite show. When you establish some sort of recurring feature or features on your blog—say an advice column, a joke page, anecdotes about silly things your baby brother said, or pictures of your dad's fashion disasters—those serve as a reason for your readers to return. And those readers will tell other readers about the blog. And they, in turn, will tell still more people, and suddenly your readership is increasing exponentially.

Many bloggers establish regular gimmicks or formulas, such as weekly columns, updated joke pages, or other specialized features, that keep people coming back for more. Here, the Clinique Fresh Faces Mobile Beauty Studio lounge hosts young customers who follow the cosmetic company's blog and Twitter feeds regarding its Fresh Faces tour.

There are many other ways of generating traffic. Use Twitter to Tweet links to your new posts. Facebook includes applications like Networked Blogs, which allows you to include your blog's RSS feed in your Facebook updates.

However, you shouldn't get ahead of yourself and assume that you're going to blow up into a huge blogging superstar overnight. That just doesn't happen. It's true that people do receive acclaim for their blogging skills. But all that "blogging skills" means, in the end, is "good writing." And good writing is, first and foremost, what you'll need to concentrate on if you want people to keep coming back to your blog to hungrily consume more of what you're serving up.

Chapter 3

Finding Your Voice as a Blogger

ow your blog is set up, and you are posting frequently. What exactly are you posting? How does your content read? Does it seem stilted and awkward, or does it flow naturally and confidently? What sort of subject matter are you blogging about? In short, have you found your voice as a blogger? And if not, how do you get to that point?

Express Yourself

So, what do you want your blog to be about? There are many kinds of blogs out there, from personal and creative writing blogs to pop culture, science, and business blogs. As a young person, you'll most likely be writing a personal blog, at least at first. Assuming that this is the case—that your blog is going to be about your life, your friends and family, and/or your personal interests and passions—your main subject matter still needs to be narrowed down quite a bit. After all, you don't want your blog to be so vague and formless that it doesn't have a distinct identity.

You may feel like one lone, isolated voice, but blogging allows you to be connected to the world at large.

In a world where literally millions of people are blogging every day, you don't just want to be another small, indistinguishable voice in all the chatter. How do you make your voice count? How will you make your writing, your opinion, and your blog stand out from the mass of other blogged opinions? What is it about your background, your expertise or special knowledge, or your writerly voice that sets you apart from the pack?

Good bloggers have a clear perspective, a consistent subject matter or focus, and a highly individual and distinctive voice. Your blogging voice should have personality, attitude, and a distinct worldview. It should be the truest expression of who you are—what you like, what you love, what makes you laugh or cry, and how you think about and see and feel the world around you.

Critical Thinking and Passionate Feeling

To hone your voice as a blogger, you need to sharpen your critical thinking skills and harness and give full expression to your passions. What does this mean? All "critical thinking" means is to think about the story, article, script, or blog that you're reading, how that piece makes you feel, what

When you watch a movie, think about how that movie made you feel and whether it worked or not and why. This is a great way to develop your critical thinking skills, which are essential skills for any blogger to possess.

the author is trying to convey, whether the author was successful in this, and whether you agree or disagree with his or her argument or main idea and its presentation

While logically analyzing how a piece is constructed, you should also remain aware of how it affects your emotions and stirs your passions (or fails to do so). When you write in your own blog about the piece you've read (or movie you've seen, or meal you've had, or video game you've played, or album you've heard), you, in turn, will be writing both critically and with passion. You will explain clearly how the thing you have experienced (book, article, blog post, movie, meal, video game, album) succeeds or doesn't succeed and why, and how it stirred your passion (or didn't).

The first thing that you need to come to grips with when critically thinking about a blog you're reading is how that blog affects you personally. What kind of impact does it have on you, and what emotions does it make you feel? Look at it this way: you are a big fan of a specific movie star. Let's call the movie star Kirk Actionface. You've seen every Kirk Actionface movie. And even though some of the films are better than others—and Kirk's had many highs and lows in his career—you're certain that his last movie was his best. The dialogue was witty, the characters were well-developed, the fight scenes were super cool, and the movie even had a few unpredictable plot twists. In fact, the movie's ending was so interesting and unpredictable that it had much in common with some of the more arty, independent films you've seen recently.

So when you get back from the movies, you hop online and go to *CinemaHipster* (a fictional name), your favorite movie blog. You are certain that *CinemaHipster*'s lead critic is going to post a four-star, hyper-enthusiastic review. But when you check out *CinemaHipster*, your face falls as you see that it has trashed the latest film, saying that it's proof Kirk Actionface's career is over. The negative review on *CinemaHipster* floors you. So what do you do? You can go to your own blog and post an angry but well-thought-out, articulate, and civil rant about how wrong *CinemaHipster*'s review is. You forcefully argue that the *CinemaHipster* critic completely misunderstood Kirk Actionface's latest opus.

In this instance, you've just given your critical thinking skills a good workout. You had no problem getting in touch with your emotions and figuring out how the *CinemaHipster* review made you feel. It ignited a fire in your belly. It made you so impassioned that you had to take to your blog immediately and pen a rebuttal to that obviously misguided review. This is Critical Thinking 101, and it's what gives your blog posts real spark and heat.

Linking Up

One of the great things about blogging is that, since it's a Web-based format, you can use the Web's great utility belt of tools to help communicate your ideas and enthusiasms. Take hyperlinks (often just called "links"), for example. On your blogroll, you can provide direct hyperlinks to other blogs. This really gives you a sense that you're part of a blogging community. Not only does it expand the appeal of your blog, but it reveals to your readers other bloggers with a similar voice.

Of course, you're not limited to linking to other blogs. You can also provide links to Web sites. Let's say that you're writing about a stand-up comedian you really like. You could provide a direct link to that comedian's Web site within your post about the comedian's newest movie. Your links can be a way to express your individuality and your personal interests, the very things that make you unique. For example, if you really like a movie—perhaps it's the latest offering from Kirk Actionface's frequent costar and love interest, Romantica DeComedy—you can make a picture of Romantica's movie poster a hyperlink. That way, when your readers click on the poster, they'll be taken to a Romantica DeComedy fan site. Using just a few simple links, you've branched out and opened up a wider, more compelling world for your readers to explore.

When people read posts like the one you've written defending the Kirk Actionface movie, even if they completely disagree with you, they'll respect your passion, honesty, and conviction. In other words, they'll see that your writing is direct. There is an element of truth to it, something that people can relate to. A voice. But how is that voice communicating itself?

Elements of Style

Another important aspect to developing a good critical voice is considering what writing style will be most appropriate for you when writing your blog. Writers' styles are conveyed by the ideas they put across, the characters they create, the tone of their stories, and their word choices.

Spending time in a library soaking up the literary talent and distinct voices of accomplished authors is a great way to help you develop and deepen your own authorial and blogging voice.

Think about your tone and word choices. When you're trying to tell your readers that the *CinemaHipster* critic is wrong about Kirk Actionface's latest movie, what is the best, most convincing way to get this across? Should you be meek and simply say that you are not sure that you agree, but it's no big deal, and the *CinemaHipster* critic has a right to his opinions? Or should you be more direct and passionate? Should you say that the *CinemaHipster* critic was so wrong in his opinion that he must have slept through the film and, in desperation to provide something to his readers who were anticipating his take on Kirk Actionface's latest blockbuster, posted some reheated version of an old review of some other, truly lame action movie?

As you can see from the examples above, a mild-mannered blogger will choose a different set of words to voice his/her opinion than will a more passionate, spirited blogger. A strong, strident, and opinionated voice will help you stand out in the blogosphere, but don't be obnoxious for the sake of attracting attention. And never be abusive. If you're passionate about something, express that passion honestly, articulately, and respectfully. Don't try to whip up a fake passion and angry rant for every topic just to entertain readers or live up to some blogger persona or self-image that you've created.

Chapter 4

Blogging Netiquette

So far, we've dealt with what sort of subject matter you should tackle on your blog, how to hone your writerly voice, and how to set up a blog. But what sort of material should you be careful about tackling? What material should you refrain from writing about entirely? And how should you behave while online? How should you behave when confronted with genuine rudeness or offensive behavior from others? In this chapter, you'll learn the answers to these questions. Here, you'll encounter the world of "netiquette," the etiquette or manners that people are expected to observe while communicating on the Internet.

Being a Responsible and Respectful Blogger

Because the Internet is such a powerful communicative tool, it's important for you to observe certain rules of conduct while blogging. Remember, your blog may potentially be seen by millions of people worldwide. Even if your readers number in the dozens rather than millions, however, you still need to consider the sensitivities of your audience and always respect the feelings of anyone you may be writing about.

If you're posting pictures of your friends, family members, or significant other on your blog, make sure you have permission before sharing any images with the public.

If you're in a romantic relationship with someone, and you mention that person in your blog, it's your responsibility to show him or her what you've written before you post it. Similarly, if you're posting pictures of your boyfriend or girlfriend, make sure you have permission to post them before sharing them with the public. If not, you may offend or embarrass your significant other. You also run the risk of damaging your relationship with that person. And never post any lewd or suggestive photos of yourself, your

DANGER IN THE BLOGOSPHERE

Danger in the Blogosphere

While many of the comments you receive on your blog will be fun to read, informative, and even flattering, some will be off-topic or cruel. You have to police your blog, looking for trolls. In blogging slang, a troll is someone who posts upsetting and often irrelevant comments to blogs. Trolls often do this to try and make you, the blogger, angry or upset. If they succeed in this, they've won. Your job is to make sure they don't succeed. You can do this by (a) not letting their silly comments get to you and (b) by moderating the comments and deleting all comments that come from trolls or other troublemakers.

Be careful about the amount of personal information you give out on the Web. There are people in cyberspace who will use this information for their own unsavory purposes. For example, there are online predators who can use the personal or identifying information that people post to stalk and possibly attack victims or steal their identities. Refrain from placing the following information online: your Social Security number, birth date, birthplace, home address, phone number(s), mother's maiden name, bank account numbers, and password(s). Also avoid posting any other information or clues that you use to remind yourself of your passwords or to identify yourself to banks or other financial institutions. You should also never give out the personal information of any bloggers you know.

Unfortunately, there are many racist, misogynistic, anti-Semitic, and homophobic blogs out there. Some bloggers use the blogosphere to spread their message of hate, fear, and intolerance. Usually, these folks are easy to spot: they live in a fearful and hysterical world of conspiracy theories that have little or no basis in reality, and their blogs reflect that. Just avoid these bloggers.

boyfriend or girlfriend, or anyone else. Photos can quickly "go viral" and be viewed and forwarded by thousands or even millions of people. By posting inappropriate images online, you may even be breaking pornography laws and risk jail time.

Your love life is not the only relationship you need to guard closely when blogging. You should also take care not to say things that will offend your family, friends, classmates, teachers, and coworkers (if you have a job). This means that you should not insult their appearance, their manner-isms, their ethnicity or race, their political or religious beliefs, or their place of work. Think of what would happen if your uncle Stu, your favorite uncle, the guy who first taught you how to ride a bike without training wheels, saw that you wrote a venomous rant on your blog about how awful the food at Chicken Shack is. The problem? Uncle Stu is the regional manager at Chicken Shack's corporate headquarters. Do you see how this could make things awkward for Uncle Stu at work, how it could threaten any chances for him to get a promotion, and how it could ruin your friendship with your favorite uncle?

It's true that blogging can be a good way to vent your anger and frustration, but it's also true that you have to choose your battles. You should practice this self-control exercise: Whenever you're about to punch the "Publish" button on a new post, take a second and think about whether you're writing that post primarily for your audience or for yourself. As a blog-ger, you're making yourself into a "public figure" of sorts, not unlike anyone else who tells stories for a mass audience (e.g., an author, comedian, talk show host, actor, etc.). Your first priority should be toward your audience. If you're just writing this post to please yourself or purge yourself of anger and annoyance, it's possible that it will hurt others. That kind of post may belong in an off-line diary, the kind no one else would see.

And remember, blogging isn't mainly about being outrageous and venting anger and spewing toxic snark. It's about sharing one's passions and enthusiasms with a community of like-minded readers. It's about sharing the best part of yourself with those who will recognize the positive value of what you have to say.

Flame-Free Commentary

Similarly, when you comment on other people's blogs, you should take a moment and think about the following question: am I posting something because it's my genuine opinion, or am I posting it just to be snarky and cruel? If it's the latter, you shouldn't post your comment. This is because there's a fine line between commenting and flaming.

Flames, or verbal attacks, are unfortunately quite common in the blogosphere. They're also quite hurtful and upsetting.

Flames, or verbal attacks, are quite common in the blogosphere. Things that people would be too shy to say to your face are things that they may be emboldened to say to you under the cover of anonymity that the Internet provides. The same may be true of you. You may feel that it's OK to leave a very cruel comment on someone else's blog. After all, it's just a blog, and it's not like you're saying it in person. Don't fool yourself. It's just as hurtful to post personal, insulting flames on someone's blog as it is to say the same things to that person in "real life."

Always take a moment to think before you respond to someone's blog post. Words have power—and they have the power to hurt. If you write something that brings your emotions to a boil, here's a tip: save it as a draft

Blogging is an ever-evolving form of communication, literature, and storytelling. But it's not the only way to open yourself up to readers or viewers. Some people also use live Webcasting, video blogging, and Twitter to communicate with the world, as this "lifecaster" is doing.

and think about it for a day or so. Return to it and see if you still think it should be posted as is. This kind of cooling-off period ensures that emotion doesn't cloud your judgment as a writer. It helps prevent you from writing anything you may soon come to regret. And you may regret an ill-advised post forever because it could very well remain accessible in cyberspace for all time.

The New Blogging Frontier

On the whole, because blogging can and should be a healthy, cathartic, and fun exercise in communication and storytelling, you also want to make sure it's a safe and secure activity as well.

Blogging is still evolving as a form of communication, storytelling, and literature. As a young blogger, you're fortunate to be at the forefront of this new frontier. There's a vast expanse of uncharted territory out there. As with the early days of sound recording, film, radio, television, and video games, right now people are still figuring out what can be done with blogging. What new stories can be told? What new formats can be explored? If you use your blogging power wisely and responsibly, and if you work hard and blog often to make your voice heard, perhaps you'll even be one of the cyberpioneers who'll answer some of these fundamental questions about the emerging art and practice of blogging.

TEN GREAT QUESTIONS
TO ASK A VETERAN BLOGGER

1 What can I do if someone online tries to provoke me into an argument?

2 If I'm writing a politically themed blog, how serious should my tone be?

3 How specialized should my blog be? Should I try to grab the largest audience possible or focus on a niche group that is interested in a particular subject?

4 What should I do if no one is reading my blog, even if I'm trying hard to increase awareness of it?

5 Why do some blogs look much flashier than others? How can I make mine look more professional?

6 Why do people say things to you online that they wouldn't say to you in person?

7 Can you change the tone or subject matter of your blog if you get bored with it?

8 Are there any guilds, or professional organizations, for bloggers?

9 How can I prevent or stop nasty exchanges among readers from occurring in my comments section?

10 How can I explain to my friends that their cruel remarks on other people's blogs aren't helping my blog at all (and, in fact, are making me uncomfortable)?

GLOSSARY

archive A collection of records or primary source documents. As a blogger, you'll usually sort your blog posts into an archive. The posts will be sorted by date, to help readers (and you) find older information more easily.

arduous Painful or difficult.

blogosphere The entire community of all blogs and their interconnections.

blogroll A list of other noteworthy blogs.

bullying The act of intimidating someone, to make that person do something he or she wouldn't ordinarily do. Bullying can include actions that are physical and/or verbal, such as violent behavior, exclusion, threats, gossip, and body language. It can also occur online, when it is known as cyberbullying.

candor The quality of being open, frank, and honest in expressing oneself to others.

comments Short text messages, used to respond to blog posts.

coveted Desired by many.

cyberspace A worldwide system of computer networks, in which online communication takes place. The term "cyberspace" is frequently used to describe the Internet.

demographic A particular section of the population, defined by its age, income, race, ethnicity, religion, sex, or other distinguishing and identifying characteristics.

enterprising Showing a willingness to try new things, take on new projects, set and meet goals, and find creative solutions to problems.

inherent Existing within someone or something as a necessary and characteristic quality or attribute.

musings Thoughts or contemplations.

phenomenon A remarkable fact, event, circumstance, or occurrence.

post Each and every time you update your blog with new text or images, you're creating a blog post, or entry, which you then add to the blog.

RSS feeds RSS (Really Simple Syndication) feeds are a simple way to syndicate, or distribute, your content (e.g., blog posts and podcasts) to your Web audience.

software The information and programs used to direct the operation of a computer.

template A framework designed to enhance the appearance of a blog.

FOR MORE INFORMATION

The Alliance for Young Artists and Writers
Scholastic Art & Writing Awards
557 Broadway
New York, NY 10012
Web site: http://www.artandwriting.org
The Alliance for Young Artists & Writers, a nonprofit organization, identi-
    fies teenagers with exceptional artistic and literary talent and brings
    their work to a national audience through the Scholastic Art &
    Writing Awards.

Canadian Internet Project (CIP)
Ryerson University School of Radio and Television Arts
Toronto, ON M5B 2K3
Canada
(416) 979-5000, ext.7549
Web site: http://www.ciponline.ca
The Canadian Internet Project (CIP) is a Ryerson University–based, long-running
    research project centering on Internet usage, trends, attitudes, and
    many other factors in our relationship with the Web.

Family Online Safety Institute
815 Connecticut Avenue, Suite 220
Washington, DC 20006
(202) 572-6252
Web site: http://www.fosi.org
The Family Online Safety Institute is an international, nonprofit organization
    that works to develop a safer Internet for children and families. It works
    to influence public policies and educate the public.

Get Net Wise
Internet Education Foundation
1634 I Street NW
Washington, DC 20009
Web site: http://www.getnetwise.org
Get Net Wise is part of the Internet Education Foundation, which works to
   provide a safe online environment for children and families.

International Technology Education Association (ITEA)
1914 Association Drive, Suite 201
Reston, VA 20191-1539
(703) 860-2100
Web site: http://www.iteaconnect.org
The International Technology Education Association promotes technology
   education and literacy.

Internet Keep Safe Coalition
1401 K Street NW, Suite 600
Washington, DC 20005
(866) 794-7233
Web site: http://www.ikeepsafe.org
The Internet Keep Safe Coalition is an educational resource for children and
   families that educates about Internet safety and ethics associated with
   Internet technologies.

The Internet Society (ISOC)
1775 Wiehle Avenue, Suite 201
Reston, VA 20190-5108
(703) 439-2120
Web site: http://www.isoc.org
The ISOC is a nonprofit organization that concentrates on maintaining high
   standards for Internet infrastructure and promotes education and govern-
   ment policies that promote open online environments.

i-SAFE Inc.
5900 Pasteur Court, Suite 100
Carlsbad, CA 92008
(760) 603-7911
Web site: http://www.isafe.org
Founded in 1998, i-SAFE Inc. is the leader in Internet safety education.
Available in all fifty states, Washington, D.C., and Department of
Defense schools located across the world, i-SAFE is a nonprofit foun-
dation whose mission is to educate and empower youth to make their
Internet experiences safe and responsible. The goal is to educate stu-
dents on how to avoid dangerous, inappropriate, or unlawful online
behavior.

Kenyon Review Young Writers Workshop
Finn House
102 West Wiggin Street
Kenyon College
Gambier, OH 43022
(740) 427-5208
Web site: htt[://www.kenyonreview.org/workshops-ywinfo.php
Young Writers is an intensive two-week workshop for intellectually curious,
motivated high-school students who value writing. Its goal is to help
students develop their creative and critical abilities with language—to
become better, more productive writers and more insightful thinkers.
The program is sponsored by the *Kenyon Review*, one of the country's
preeminent literary magazines.

Media Awareness Network
1500 Merivale Road, 3rd Floor
Ottawa, ON K2E6Z5
Canada
(613) 224-7721
Web site: http://www.media-awareness.ca

The Media Awareness Network creates media literacy programs for young people. The site contains educational games about the Internet and the media.

NetSmartz
Charles B. Wang International Children's Building
699 Prince Street
Alexandria, VA 22314-3175
(800) 843-5678
Web site: http://www.netsmartz.org
NetSmartz provides children, teens, and parents resources to help educate young people about how to surf the Internet safely.

Weekly Reader Publishing
Weekly Reader's Student Publishing Contest
3001 Cindel Drive
Delran, NJ 08075
(800) 446-3355
Web site: http://www.weeklyreader.com
Weekly Reader's Student Publishing Contest honors the nation's best nonfiction writing by students in grades three to twelve. Individual pieces as well as print and online student publications are eligible. Winners receive a free trip to Washington, D.C., plus other prizes.

Web Sites

Due to the changing nature of Internet links, Rosen Publishing has developed an online list of Web sites related to the subject of this book. This site is updated regularly. Please use this link to access this list:

http://www.rosenlinks.com/dil/blog

FOR FURTHER READING

Bailey, Diane. *Cyber Ethics.* New York, NY: Rosen Central, 2008.

Banks, Michael A. *Blogging Heroes: Interviews With 30 of the World's Top Bloggers.* Indianapolis, IN: Wiley Publishing, Inc., 2008.

Douglas, Nick. *Twitter Wit: Brilliance in 140 Characters or Less.* New York, NY: HarperCollins, 2009.

Freeman-Zachery, Rice. *Creative Time and Space: Making Room for Making Art.* Cincinnatti, OH: North Light Books, 2010.

Frey, Tara. *Blogging for Bliss: Crafting Your Own Online Journal: A Guide for Crafters, Artists, & Creatives of All Kinds.* New York, NY: Lark Books, 2009.

Furgang, Kathy. *Netiquette: A Student's Guide to Digital Etiquette* (Digital and Information Literacy). New York, NY: Rosen Central, 2011.

Gaynor, Sheri. *Creative Awakenings: Envisioning the Life of Your Dreams Through Art.* Cincinnatti, OH: North Light Books, 2009.

Gunelius, Susan. *Blogging All-In-One for Dummies.* Indianapolis, IN: Wiley Publishing, Inc., 2010.

Handley, Ann, and C. C. Chapman. *Content Rules: How to Create Killer Blogs, Podcasts, Videos, Ebooks, Webinars (and More) That Engage Customers and Ignite Your Business.* Hoboken, NJ: John Wiley & Sons, Inc., 2011.

Hile, Lori. *Social Networks and Blogs* (Mastering Media). Chicago, IL: Heinemann Raintree, 2010.

Hussey, Tris. *Using Wordpress.* Upper Saddle River, NJ: Pearson Education Inc., 2011.

Lerer, Kenneth, Arianna Huffington, and the editors of the *Huffington Post. The Huffington Post Complete Guide to Blogging.* New York, NY: Simon & Schuster, 2008.

Majure, Janet. *Teach Yourself Visually: WordPress.* Indianapolis, IN: Wiley Publishing, Inc., 2010.

Micek, Deborah, and Warren Whitlock. *Twitter Revolution: How Social Media and Mobile Marketing Is Changing the Way We Do Business and Market Online.* Las Vegas, NV: Xeno Press, 2008.

Pearl, Nancy. *Book Crush: For Kids and Teens—Recommended Reading for Every Mood, Moment, and Interest.* Seattle, WA: Sasquatch Books, 2007.

Reeder, Joelle, and Katherine Scoleri. *The IT Girl's Guide to Blogging with Moxie.* Hoboken, NJ: John Wiley & Sons, Inc., 2007.

Rowse, Darren, and Chris Garrett. *ProBlogger: Secrets for Blogging Your Way to a Six-Figure Income.* Indianapolis, IN: Wiley Publishing, Inc., 2010.

Sabin-Wilson, Lisa. *WordPress for Dummies.* Indianapolis, IN: Wiley Publishing, Inc., 2010.

Willard, Nancy. *Cyberbullying and Cyberthreats: Responding to the Challenge of Online Social Aggression, Threats, and Distress.* Champaign, IL: Research Press, 2007.

BIBLIOGRAPHY

Blood, Rebecca. *The Weblog Handbook*. New York, NY: Basic Books, 2002.

Crace, John. "The Teen Bloggers Who Took Over the Internet." *The Guardian*, September 9, 2009. Retrieved April 2011 (http://www.guardian.co.uk/technology/2009/sep/09/teenage-bloggers).

Doctorow, Cory. "Digital Media Literacy for Kids." Boingboing.net, May 25, 2011. Retrieved May 2011 (http://www.boingboing.net/2011/05/25/digital-media-litera.html).

Gardner, Susannah, and Shane Birley. *Blogging for Dummies*. Hoboken, NJ: John Wiley & Sons, Inc., 2010.

Gosney, John W. *Blogging for Teens*. Boston, MA: Thomson Course Technology PTR, 2004.

Hussey, Tris. *Create Your Own Blog: 6 Easy Projects to Start Blogging Like a Pro*. Indianapolis, IN: Sams Publishing, 2010.

Kwan, Amanda. "Young Fashion Bloggers Are Worrisome Trend to Parents." *USA Today*, August 13, 2008. Retrieved April 2011 (http://www.usatoday.com/tech/webguide/internetlife/2008-08-12-girl-fashion-blogs_N.htm).

Lewinski, John Scott. "Diablo Cody's Tips for Blogging Your Way to Hollywood Success." Wired.com, November 16, 2007. Retrieved May 2011 (http://www.wired.com/entertainment/hollywood/news/2007/11/cody).

Luhtala, Michelle. "What's Blocked in Schools? A Whole Lot!" Bibliotech.me, April 22, 2011. Retrieved May 2011 (http://mluhtala.blogspot.com/2011/04/whats-blocked-in-schools-whole-lot.html).

Nelson, Melanie. "Choosing Typepad as Your Blogging Platform." BloggingBasics101.com, January 26, 2009. Retrieved April 2011 (http://www.bloggingbasics101.com/2009/01/choosing-typepad-as-your-blogging-platform).

Nelson, Melanie. "Choosing Wordpress as Your Blogging Platform." BloggingBasics101.com, February 4, 2009. Retrieved April 2011 (http://www.bloggingbasics101.com/2009/02/choosing-wordpress-as-your-blogging-platform).

Nelson, Melanie. "How Do I Choose a Blogging Platform?" BloggingBasics101.com, January 21, 2009. Retrieved April 2011 (http://www.bloggingbasics101.com/2009/01/choosing-a-blogging-platform).

Nelson, Melanie. "How Do I Start a Blog?" BloggingBasics101.com, April 14, 2008. Retrieved April 2011 (http://www.bloggingbasics101.com/2008/04/how-do-i-start).

Nelson, Melanie. "Using Blogger (Blogspot) as Your Blogging Platform." BloggingBasics101.com, January 22, 2009. Retrieved April 2011 (http://www.bloggingbasics101.com/2009/01/using-blogger-blogspot-as-your-blogging-platform).

Normile, Nick. "2010 Hierarchy of Halloween Candy." Foodie at Fifteen, November 1, 2010. Retrieved April 2011 (http://foodieatfifteen.blogspot.com/2010/11/2010-hierarchy-of-halloween-candy.html).

Porter, Joshua. "Nine Lessons for Would-Be Bloggers." Blog Soup, April 4, 2007. Retrieved May 2011 (http://www.techsoup.org/learningcenter/internet/page6724.cfm).

Riley, Marcus. "Famous Teen Fashion Blogger to Make Chicago Appearance." NBCChicago.com, February 3, 2011. Retrieved April 2011 (http://www.nbcchicago.com/the-scene/fashion/Tavi-Gevinson-the-interview-show-mark-bazer-style-rookie-115213144.html).

Roth, E. "How Do You Do Squarespace? The Order of St. Andrew." Squarespace, April 12, 2011. Retrieved May 2011 (http://blog.squarespace.com/blog/2011/4/12/how-do-you-squarespace-the-order-of-st-andrew.html).

Seger, Linda. *Making a Good Writer Great: A Creativity Workbook for Screenwriters.* Beverly Hills, CA: Silman-James Press, 1999.

Wagner, Hank, Christopher Golden, and Stephen R. Bissette. *Prince of Stories: The Many Worlds of Neil Gaiman.* New York, NY: St. Martin's Press, 2008.

Wheaton, Wil. *Just a Geek.* Sebastopol, CA: O'Reilly Media, Inc., 2004.

INDEX

About the Author

Arie Kaplan is an author, comic book writer, and screenwriter who has blogged for such Web sites as AMCtv.com and MyJewishLearning.com. In addition, Arie is a video game writer, and he has written the story and dialogue for the licensed *House M.D.* video game, out now from Legacy Interactive. He's also the author of the Disney Club Penguin graphic novel *Shadow Guy & Gamma Gal: Heroes Unite* (Grosset & Dunlap, 2010), which is set in the world of the Club Penguin massively multiplayer online role-playing game. Arie's other Rosen Publishing books include *Dracula: The Life of Vlad the Impaler* and the forthcoming *A Young Man's Guide to Contemporary Issues: Dating and Relationships: Navigating the Social Scene*. Arie is an in-demand public speaker who travels all over the world to lecture about the history of comedy, the history of television, film history, comic book history, and other pop culture–related subjects. Aside from his work as a writer for DC Comics, *MAD Magazine*, Archie Comics, IDW Publishing, and Bongo Comics, Arie is the author of the critically acclaimed nonfiction book *From Krakow to Krypton: Jews and Comics* (Jewish Publication Society, 2008).

Photo Credits

Cover (background) and interior graphics © www.istockphoto.com/suprun; cover, p. 1 (left to right) © www.istockphoto.com/Justin Allfree, © www.istockphoto.com/George Peters, © www.istockphoto.com/Goldmund Lukic, © www.istockphoto.com/Slobodan Vasic; pp. 5, 23 Fuse/Getty Images; p. 7 Heather Charles/Chicago Tribune/MCT via Getty Images; p. 8 http://en.wikipedia.org/wiki/File:Jornbarger.JPG; p. 10 Peter Dazeley/Photographer's Choice/Getty Images; p. 15 William Andrew/Photographer's Choice/Getty Images; p. 16 Shutterstock; p. 18 Scott Dunlap/iStock Vectors/Getty Images; p. 21 Mark Von Holden/Getty Images for Clinique; p. 24 Emmanuel Faure/Stone/Getty Images; p. 27 Image Source/Getty Images; p. 30 Jenny Acheson/Stockbyte/Thinkstock; p. 33 Hemera/Thinkstock; p. 34 Rodger Mallison/Fort Worth Star-Telegram/MCT via Getty Images.

Designer: Nicole Russo; Photo Researcher: Amy Feinberg